Securing Your Internet Life

A Step By Step Guide to Secure Yourself Online

Table of Contents

Introduction

I want to thank you and congratulate you for purchasing the book, "Securing Your Internet Life

A Step By Step Guide to Secure Yourself Online."

It's a well-known fact that scouring through the online world not just conveys accommodation to the world all in all, however there are numerous things that you can do online today that you couldn't do a few years prior. Not just would you be able to now shop online for all intents and purposes anything that you require, yet you can enter the universe of dating, meet new companions and even look for some kind of employment on the web.

With the online world we now can stay associated with the whole world without leaving the solace of our own homes. All that you need is a PC and you are set to go. But, as helpful as this world might be, regardless it represents its own Extraordinary arrangement of perils.

Living behind the dividers of a PC won't abandon you mysterious and there is tremendous danger included with regards to keeping the greater part of your own data avoided the individuals who might hurt it.

It is fantastically simple to find a man today utilizing a PC, that all you truly need is a name and a location. Albeit numerous individuals today would censure the demonstration of staying mysterious online as the main individuals who do that are the individuals who more often than not partake in illicit matter, there is a way that you can stay unknown and safe while scouring the Internet.

In this book you will discover a rundown of arrangements and tips that will help you to stay private online and every one of them are moderately easy to take after. In the event that you are searching for an approach to secure yourself on the web, this is positively the book for you.

Thanks again for downloading this book, I hope you enjoy it!

Chapter 1: How to Be Anonymous on the Internet

Anyway, what is secrecy by definition? The demonstration of obscurity is the capacity to keep the greater part of your activities, exercises or genuine personality safe and from being known openly. There are various reasons why a wide range of substances that we experience on the Internet today need to discover your actual character keeping in mind the end goal to discover why you buys certain articles on the web, track past buys and in addition other searching exercises.

While these elements are more often than not totally innocuous, it is not extraordinary for law implementation authorities to find somebody's genuine personality particularly if that individual has been already connected to a wrongdoing. A large portion of us as of now have a particular character to which we pass by as of now and we are known as by our companions, family, banks and government by a particular name and nom de plume.

These individuals can without much of a stretch distinguish us by our government managed savings number, the photograph on our driver's permit, sound history or notoriety. We as a whole have some sort of open personality to which we pass by and the fact of the matter is the greater part of us abstain from keeping ourselves mysterious essentially out of need.

Why do this? It is on the grounds that it is simply helpful. Anonymity is a long way from advantageous and there are times where all we need is accommodation. Who wouldn't like to do a straightforward Google pursuit or check their email account without going through the inconvenience of concealing who they truly are? Try not to feel terrible for needing comfort, in any case, don't accept that you will never have the capacity to do anything secretly.

Utilizing the right web programs or records will permit you to advantageously do everything that you want to do while on the Internet, while as yet keeping your obscurity in place. While the associations and signs that you abandon at whatever point you are online being not generally took after by individuals who might utilize your data hurtfully, these breadcrumbs can even now be effortlessly found by an assortment of government offices or programmers, particularly on the off chance that they attempt keeping in mind the end goal to discover who you truly are.

With regards to obscurity, you have to start from the beginning, particularly on the off chance that you need to keep yourself safe. The most ideal approach to keep secrecy is to ensure that you keep the greater part of your records that are associated with your genuine personality separate from the records that are associated with your mysterious character.

The Levels of Anonymity

There are diverse levels of anonymity that you can accomplish and anybody can accomplish the particular level that they need the length of they are exceptionally imaginative and have entry to the greater part of the right assets. The more you do to shield your protection, the larger amount of anonymity that you will have. To best raise your level of anonymity, you first should ask yourself what particular level do you require?

Obviously to answer this inquiry you should investigate the future to foresee precisely how private you need to remain. On the off chance that you have some thought of who or what you are attempting to shield your personality from and what assets they may have available to them, you will have the capacity to authorize the best possible level of obscurity without going over the edge and squandering your own time and assets.

Tragically, there is no real way to advise precisely whom you are attempting to shield your personality from. Once in a while there are covering levels of secrecy. They aren't generally so straightforward. That discussion troll you affronted may happen to be an upper level NSA examiner with access to plentiful assets. In all actuality you never know.

Chapter 2: How to Clean Your Online Information

Before you can even begin pondering securing your way of life in general, you have to completely comprehend what data you have that is as of now promptly accessible on the web. You might be astounded to discover the amount of data there is about you online as of now.

You may discover delicate data about you waiting on the Internet today, for example, telephone number, email address, full legitimate name, birthdate and government managed savings number.

These are only a little rundown of things that ought not be online for the whole world to see and it is critical that you discover what is waiting on the Internet so you can get them down before any other person can see them. To begin searching for your touchy bits of data on the web, take after these simple strides:

What Can Others See About You?

To do this direct a basic hunt in Google, Bing or Yahoo seek. In any case, keeping in mind the end goal to do this effectively ensure you are not signed into any of your email accounts with these networks programs or online networking destinations.

On the off chance that you are marked into anything the web index will get certain action in view of the data that is put away on your PC. When you do the inquiry ensure that you take a gander at both the web and pictures classification to see precisely what you can see

Make a list of everything that you find. If you discover a ton or a little data about yourself on the web, ensure that you take notes on everything that you discover. Record everything!

At the point when ensuring that you record site data, where the data started from and other related data to the site, for example, telephone number or address in the event that they are accessible.

Removing Sensitive Information

On the off chance that by chance you have an extensive rundown of sites that contain your name or other individual data on it, the best thing that you can do is to begin off with the most fundamental sites.

Why would you do this? Since these little sites could have gotten your data off of other greater sites, for example, Google or Facebook.

Secure Social Networking

The vast majority don't understand that each time they upgrade their timetable or profile in Facebook, web indexes are instantly cautioned and rank the new data that it gets. However, there is an approach to ensure this doesn't keep happening for you and all that you need to do is change the security settings inside you profile.

To do this Unlink your timetable from web indexes by killing the "Who can find me?" highlight. Observe that after you killed this component, it might take some time, as a rule 24 to 48 hours, for the internet searcher to execute it, so regardless you may see your Facebook profile on the query items.

Learn more about the google plus account. With 'Google+' accounts, there is no real way to make your profile private starting now – and it appears like Google doesn't have any arrangements to include that element later on – so all the better you can do is put a confinement on it, constraining general society to seeing just your name and profile picture.

The choice to erase your entire 'Google+' profile is additionally accessible, however don't stress, erasing your open profile does not influence your Gmail account, on the off chance that you have one. Disabling accounts and adding restrictions confinements or should be possible under the settings Page.

Protecting Your Data

The minute that you evacuate the greater part of your own and delicate data disconnected from the net, it is then your obligation to guarantee that your information stays off the Internet no matter what.

There are various ways that you can do this and in the following couple of sections you will figure out how this can be accomplished.

Chapter 3: Online Privacy

In the event that you have not heard of an IP address it just stands for The Internet Protocol Address. This location is basically a one of a kind arrangement of numbers that distinguishes your particular PC on the whole system that is known as the Internet. To place it in straightforward terms, your IP location is your location that is utilized as a part of the virtual world. Without it, you can't do a thing.

While your IP address does not have data that can tell some individual that you are the individual that claims the IP address or that can give away the greater part of your own data, there are sure ways that organizations can get data on you. Under specific laws all through the US an office can demand to have your own data specifically from your Internet Service Provider.

On the off chance that there are lawful papers displayed, your administration supplier won't have any decision yet to hand over your data. The vast majority don't have an issue with certain genuine organizations from asking for their data, however we are surely not one of those individuals. Offices are not by any means the only individuals out there who need my data or yours. There are other individuals, for example, stalkers, tricksters and programmers that need the data too and they are simply staying there sneaking out of sight, sitting tight for their opportunity to get that data.

Cookies

What is A Cookie? How can it assume a part in how safe you are online?

Cookies are vital bits of data that are put away in your PC naturally from the various sites that you have gone by or that you are signed into. These little bits of data could contain individual data about you, for example, your login data, what your client inclinations are and what sort of exchanges you have made online before.

A Cookie makes a site recall who you are each time you come back to them, which makes it less demanding for you to sign onto a site each time you return. This is likewise the essential motivation behind why you may see significant results on your pursuits.

There are two essential sorts of cookies that you will go over online: outsider cookies and first gathering cookies.

- First Party Cookies - These are ones that come straightforwardly from the numerous sites that you have gone by.
- Outsider Cookies - These sorts of treats as a rule originate from any sort of partnered destinations that you have gone by previously. Regularly these are publicists or promoters that work online that have a concurrence with your most loved sites, for example, YouTube, Facebook or Instagram.

At whatever point you agree to another site, more often than not inside the fine print you will find that your most loved site is permitted to hand over your own data to alternate sites they are banded together with.

More often than not though, the main ones who have a tendency to have your data and will be the most irksome to you are programmers and con artists.

Be Anonymous on Your Computer

Since you completely see how your own data can be acquired basically by doing basic errands online, for example, going to your most loved site or shopping, the time has come to take in the best heading to use keeping in mind the end goal to push ahead with your online secrecy.

- **Search the Internet Using the Private Setting or The Incognito Setting**

  One of the most widely recognized recommendations you'll get when you need to peruse secretly is to utilize private scanning or the in disguise method of your favored web programs. When you're "private" scanning, the program does not record any of the locales you chat, so it doesn't show up on your hunt history.

Be that as it may, it doesn't keep these went by locales from recording your log and catching the data you entered, if there is any. Essentially, private skimming just shields you from the following individual who's going to utilize the PC, as they may gaze upward your inquiry history.

- **Utilizing Web-Based Proxies**

Every time you open a web program, sort a site address, and press enter, you are sending a solicitation to the web server to give you a chance to get to the webpage. For the web server to send back the page you asked for, it needs your IP address. With this sort of framework, it is difficult to hush up about IP addresses; in any case, there is a strategy that will conceal it.

Utilizing web intermediary servers does this. A web intermediary server is a delegate between a client's PC and the web. While getting to the Internet, a client's PC will first associate with the web intermediary server, and the web intermediary server will then send the solicitation to the site the client wishes to be associated with, subsequently concealing the individual's IP address. What the site will see is the intermediary server's IP address. There are two diverse ways that you can utilize electronic intermediary servers:

- o Designing your program physically keeping in mind the end goal to get to these intermediary servers.
- o Use sites that are web intermediaries to get to confined sites.

- **Utilize the Tor Also Known as The Onion Router**

The main question that you should ask yourself is what is Tor in any case? Tor is really a standout amongst the best ways that you can peruse the Internet secretly. The Onion Router, or as it is most normally alluded to as Tor, is a product that is totally allowed to utilize and that helps you to keep up anonymity when perusing on the web.

This product can oppose both system and land control. In view of its ability the legislature has regarded it unsafe as it can construct a pathway in some illicit exercises, for example, terrorism, drug managing, erotica and arms managing.

While it has increased such notoriety, the makers accentuate that the product is made for informants, activists, columnists, militaries, law requirement officers, and other individuals who have related vocations, which may imperil one's life, particularly in the event that one is living in a nation with an onerous government.

From a large portion of a million, Tor had an enormous increment in its number of clients after it was uncovered to the general population by the US and UK spies about the conceivable issues this project could make. Their everyday clients expanded to four million in only a year. To run Tor all you need is a Mac, Linux PC, or Windows PC, in the event that you are hoping to look after anonymity.

The Tor programming works by with encryption, clients are just ready to shroud the substance of the message, yet not the headers. Headers are the data where a message started and where it was sent. It can likewise incorporate the data of the record size sent or asked for and the accurate time of these exercises. In view of this data, an online observation framework utilizing refined activity examination may have a high likelihood of foreseeing the substance of your message.

Message, in this sense, alludes to your online movement. To place it in basic terms, consider how you would lose somebody that is tailing you. Wouldn't you need to take distinctive courses keeping in mind the end goal to lose this individual? All things considered, Tor works the same way.

- **Utilizing Anonymous E-mail Accounts**

  When it comes to utilizing unknown email addresses, regardless of the fact that you surrender fake data, which in any case does not keep your IP address covered up.

  What does this mean? It essentially implies that you can be followed and your own data can in any case be found. In the event that the administration was worried about your Internet exercises and asked for your data, they could get it effortlessly. To keep this from happening, the best thing that you can do is make a fake-email address utilizing the Tor program.

  At the point when you are checking these messages you ought to dependably utilize Tor particularly on the off chance that you don't need your IP address uncovered.

Creating an Anonymous Email Account

While making your fake email account, don't utilize Google or Yahoo. Google does not permit mysterious individuals to join. Yippee does not bolster HTTPS insurance. Tor and HTTPS ought to go as an inseparable unit for a man to be really unknown.

Here are the particular strides to making a fake email address utilizing your Tor program:

- Open up the Tor program.
- Get to either the MailTor or Mail2Tor administration that is covered up inside it. These two will serve as your essential email suppliers.
- Make a record on both of these two destinations. Nonetheless, ensure that you don't list any data that could be connected to your actual character. Make up everything.
- At whatever point you send messages, ensure that any of the substance inside the email can't be connected back to you in any capacity.

Obviously it is vital for you to comprehend that every technique that you utilize has its own particular preferences and in addition its own particular restrictions.

Chapter 4: Security

Email Encryption

Encryption transforms your email into a code that must be deciphered with a key, then sends it to the beneficiary, who can just read it on the off chance that they have the same key.

Between steady breaching of passwords and the NSA looking in on all that you do, you've most likely got security on the psyche of late. In case you're searching for somewhat individual protection in your interchanges with companions and friends and family, or you simply need to trust that the reports you email to your client or accountant aren't being blocked and read, you'll have to scramble those messages. Thankfully, it's anything but difficult to do. Here's the means by which.

Encoding your email may sound overwhelming, yet it's quite basic.

It'll make your messages look like jumbled content to uninvited spectators, similar to the café packet sniffer or library SSL cracker. It'll additionally darken MasterCard numbers, addresses, photographs, and whatever else you may incline toward be private on the off chance that you don't as of now have a protected association with your email supplier.

Use Mailvelope for Gmail to do it. Mailvelope is only an expansion, so it doesn't take much time to set up.

The most concerning issue with email encryption presumably isn't you, it's the general population you send messages to. Both you and the beneficiary need the encryption programming since when you email something to somebody, they need to decode it on their end utilizing a key you send them.

This implies you have to first send them the unscrambling key by another type of correspondence like telephone or content, then they have to experience the inconvenience of decoding it on their end utilizing the same programming you did.

The vast majority of us aren't going to encode all that we send on the grounds that there's truly no reason for doing it. All things considered, sending an email to your folks requesting a news upgrade isn't generally worth encryption. Notwithstanding, sending an email to your folks requesting their standardized savings number for some structures is justified, despite all the trouble. In any case, that is it for the vast majority of us.

Like anything, email encryption has vulnerabilities, yet generally it's a safe approach to convey. It positively won't keep you out of the look of the exceptionally engaged eye of the legislature, however the 12-year-old programmer down the road presumably won't have the capacity to snoop in on your email. On the off chance that you require encryption past webmail, we prescribe the Enigmail Project.

Encrypt Your Chats

Like email, you may likewise need to scramble your text chat discussions. Additionally, like email, this is unfathomably simple to do. We set up a couple distinctive strategies for this.

Most importantly, encryption is anything but difficult to turn on in a talk customer like Adium by simply tapping on the lock symbol in a chat (Pidgin clients can get this also). This turns on Off the Record Messaging that is scrambled, validated, and not put away.

With Adium, you're setting is appended to your record (or to a particular contact) so you don't need to experience and set this up inevitably. Fundamentally, it's a "set it and overlook" technique for encryption.

Chat encryption is quite straightforward and doesn't generally have a great deal of drawbacks. The decent thing about how Adium handles it is that it just steps to set up, and after that it's on for good. The individual on the less than desirable end needs either Adium or Pidgin introduced also, however generally it's super simple. The main genuine drawback is that you likewise need to dispose of chat interpretations, which can be useful on the off chance that you have to return to discussions.

For the vast majority of us, OTR encryption is bounty. It's hard to split, and takes a considerable measure of time to do it. OTR is essentially about keeping discussions private and it benefits a vocation with it. For something considerably more dispensable and encoded, we'd additionally prescribe programming like Tor Chat or Cryptocat for gathering discussions.

Using Secure Back-up and File Sync

Whether you're utilizing an administration like Dropbox for record synchronizing or a full reinforcement like Crashplan, you don't need individuals snooping around in your private information. In like manner, document encryption is pretty much as helpful on the off chance that you have a huge amount of flat mates who you think may snoop in on your PC at home.

Encryption is quite simple to set up. Crashplan does it naturally for you, so you don't have to do anything by any means. With an administration like Dropbox, you really have a couple of choices. You can encode your documents physically before you transfer them, or utilize an administration like SafeMonk to scramble them before they're transferred.

TrueCrypt is no more a suitable arrangement, we're searching for different choices for this area. TrueCrypt makes it truly simple to scramble all that you have to, yet once it's encoded you can't utilize it from another PC or cell phone. This is fine much of the time.

There's never such a mind-bending concept as an uncrackable encryption, however TrueCrypt is dependable for securing your information. Obviously, TrueCrypt is secured with a secret key, so don't go leaving that around. In the event that you'd incline toward, you can likewise simply go totally off the matrix utilizing something like a Raspberry Pi as a Dropbox clone.

Along these lines you're the special case who even knows your record matching up administration exists. Another choice is to go from Dropbox to another distributed storage administration with encryption worked in like one of these. Changing from Dropbox over to an administration like Spideroak just takes the length of it takes to reinforcement every one of your information once more, so that is a reasonable choice also.

The advantage is that once you've done the switch you don't need to consider it any longer, however you do pass up a major opportunity for a portion of the cooperative elements Dropbox brings to the table.

Password Manager

A secret key administrator arbitrarily creates every one of your passwords for sites and bolts them behind a solitary expert watchword just you know. This implies you just need to recollect a solitary password.

LastPass is confounding to newcomers and it takes for a moment to get into utilizing it legitimately. Moreover, it's quite pointless to begin utilizing something like LastPass unless you're really going to experience and set new passwords for all your records, which can take quite a while in the event that you utilize a variety of administrations.

In the event that you bounce around between PCs, say from work to home, then you have to introduce your watchword director on every one of your frameworks. Else you will keep yourself out of records since you can't recall the secret key.

Once they're set up and going, a password director is incredible, however it takes a ton to get to that point. Actually, for a secret key administrator like LastPass, we have both an apprentice's aide and a moderate one alongside supplemental tips also. Which is to say: password administrators are mistaking for a great many people.

Any password supervisor is just as secure as your watchword, yet they're still quite solid. You'll additionally require a solid password regardless.

Chapter 5: Two-Factor Authentication

Two-factor authentication is accessible on a huge amount of administrations nowadays. Basically, it's a basic element that requests more than your password. It requires something you know (like your watchword) and something you have (like your telephone). For instance, to sign into your Google account, you'd have to sort in your watchword, sit tight for Google to send you an instant message with a code, and afterward sort that in before you could get to your record on another machine.

Two-factor authentication is one of those arrangements that sounds much more irritating than it really is by and by. When you get it set up on every one of your gadgets and administrations, it practically vanishes away from plain sight. Most administrations, as Facebook or Twitter, just require a solitary verification on every gadget. Along these lines, once you set up and confirm your character once, you're ready. Different administrations, similar to Google, oblige you to verify like clockwork. If you have your telephone with you, this takes a few seconds every time and truly isn't an issue.

Two-factor authentication is inconceivably secure on the grounds that programmers dependably require no less than two of your gadgets to get into your record. Clearly this is still conceivable, however it's more improbable that somebody will have both your telephone and your tablet than only one gadget.

How Secure Is it?

Two-factor verification signifies "something you know" (like a secret key) and "something you have," which can be an article like a telephone. We have taken a bit of times to bust a few Questions about the security of 2 factor verification. Please take a minute to read through them.

Question: But imagine a scenario where my mobile phone doesn't have SMS/flag, or I'm in an outside nation.

Answer: You can introduce a standalone application called Google Authenticator (it's likewise accessible in the App Store), so your PDA needn't bother with a sign.

Question: Okay, however shouldn't something be said about if my PDA comes up short on force, or my telephone is stolen?

Answer: You can print out a little bit of paper with 10 one-time rescue codes and place that in your wallet. Utilize those one-time codes to sign in even without your telephone.

Question: Don't I need to tinker with an additional PIN each time I sign in?

Answer: You can advise Google to believe your PC for 30 days and some of the time much more.

Question: Okay, yet imagine a scenario where I need to check how secure Google Authenticator is.

Answer: Google Authenticator is free, open-source, and in view of open measures.

Utilize an alternate password on Gmail/Google than on different administrations. On the off chance that you reuse a password and a hacker splits into one organization, they can utilize the same to break into your Google account.

Turn on Two-Factor Authentication now!

Chapter 6: Don't!

- **Utilize Basic Passwords**

  People tend to utilize basic passwords that are anything but difficult to recall like the names of dear ones and pets, birthdays or their most loved groups' names. The issue with picking such passwords is that, they can be speculated effectively or can be split inside seconds utilizing password splitting devices.

- **Forget to Remote Wipe Your Smart Phone if you Lost it**

  Many advanced cells give highlights like 'Android Lost', 'Discover My iPhone', or 'BlackBerry Protect" which let the clients remotely wipe away all the individual information on their phones, in the event that they are stolen or lost.

- **Respond to Pop-Ups**

  You should be acquainted with pop-ups that say you are the 10,000,000th guest of a site or that you have won a free iPhone and that you should simply tap on a connection to guarantee your prize. Never at any point react to such pop-ups.

- **Be Afraid to use than one email account**

  Don't utilize a solitary email represent everything. Make an email represent each reason, for instance, put aside an email represent individual sends, another for web shopping or ticket booking, one for internet managing an account, one for business related sends

Conclusion

Thank you again for downloading this book!

There will dependably be sure data that we just basically need to mind our own business in order to guarantee our own particular security. In any case, frequently our security is undermined by the individuals who increase unapproved access to both our business and individual data that we have on the web.

Keeping up individual online secrecy is a test and it is one that each individual appearance. With the advances in innovation today, it is difficult to go anyplace on the Internet where our data is not being put away, followed, copied or got to.

Regardless of what your reasons perhaps to want to go on the Internet secretly, we as a whole have the privilege to battle for our protection, whether it is out in broad daylight or in the computerized world. The data that is put away online while might be microscopic, yet it can in any case can possibly hurt us over the long haul and is regularly on sold to different organizations that desire to have it.

I trust that by utilizing this book you will have the capacity to begin keeping your protection the way you are qualified for and can begin on the way towards keeping up your secrecy.

Finally, if you enjoyed this book, please take the time to share your thoughts and post a review on Amazon. It'd be greatly appreciated!

Thank you and good luck!

www.ingramcontent.com/pod-product-compliance
Lightning Source LLC
Chambersburg PA
CBHW060936050326
40689CB00013B/3118